GUESTHOUSE

by Nicola Werenowska

Published by Playdead Press 2018

© Nicola Werenowska 2018

Nicola Werenowska has asserted her rights under the Copyright, Design and Patents Act, 1988, to be identified as the authors of this work.

A CIP catalogue record for this book is available from the British Library.

ISBN 978-1-910067-65-9

Caution
All rights whatsoever in this play are strictly reserved and application for performance should be sought through the author before rehearsals begin. No performance may be given unless a license has been obtained.

This book is sold subject to the condition that it shall not by way of trade or otherwise, be lent, resold, hired out, or otherwise circulated without the publisher's prior consent in any form of binding or cover other than that in which it is published and without a similar condition including this condition being imposed on the subsequent purchaser.

Playdead Press
www.playdeadpress.com

GUESTHOUSE
by Nicola Werenowska

Val	Amanda Bellamy
Lisa	Clare Humphrey
Chloe	Eleanor Jackson
Director	Tony Casement
Designer	Anna Kelsey
Assistant Director	Valerie Christiansen
Producer	Eastern Angles Theatre Company

'*Guesthouse*' has been funded by Eastern Angles Theatre Company and Arts Council England and developed in association with the Mercury Theatre, Firstsite, Lakeside Theatre, and Essex Book Festival.

After sharings at Lakeside Theatre, West Cliff, and Hotbed Theatre Festival 2016, '*Guesthouse*' will premiere at the John Peel Centre, Stowmarket on 14 March 2018 before touring to venues across East Anglia including a week at Sir John Mills Theatre.

CAST

AMANDA BELLAMY | Val

Amanda trained at RADA and at Lecoq in Paris. She recently played Jane Wenham in *Jane Wenham, Witch of Walkern*, with Eastern Angles and at the Arcola in London. She's extremely happy to be back with Eastern Angles! Other credits include Winnie in *Happy Days* at the BAC, Esther in Arthur Miller's *The Price* for Compass Theatre; Elizabeth Bennet in *Pride and Prejudice*, Julia in *The Duchess of Malfi*, Lottie in *Good Morning Bill* and Grekova in *Platonov*, all at Salisbury Playhouse. She was Hypatia in *Misalliance* at Leatherhead, Toine in *Piaf* at Harrogate and Lady Macbeth at Manchester Contact Theatre. Other Shakespeare includes Helena in *A Midsummer Nights Dream* at Hull Truck, Hermia in John Caird's *Dream* at the RSC, Jessica in *The Merchant of Venice*, Olivia in *Twelfth Night* and Rosaline in *Love's Labours Lost*. She also played, Corinne Schroeder in Greg Doran's *Ispanka*, Maria in *Have* and Lady Haughty in Danny Boyles *Epicoene*, all at the RSC. Amanda has developed several new plays in the NT Studio and played Violette in *A Little Hotel on the Side* in the Olivier. Nine Ayckbourn's to date, include Annie in *The Norman Conquests Trilogy*; and Jane in *Absurd Person Singular*, (at Newbury Watermill). At Theatre by the Lake in Keswick, she was Peg in *Wallflowering*, Mrs Bradman, and then Madame Arcati in *Blithe Spirit* and Homily in *The Borrowers*. At Pitlochry Amanda played Poppy in A Small Family Business and Anna in *The Government Inspector*.

Television appearances include Margaret in *Hotel Trubble*, *Bunny Time* for the Disney Channel, three series as Rose in *You Rang M'Lord*, Hetty in Carla Laine's series, *Searching* and episodes of *Bergerac*, *All in Good Faith* and *Terry and June*. She was Cindy in Yorkshire TV's *Glorious Day* and played Rose in the film of *Little Dorrit*.

CLARE HUMPHREY | Lisa

Theatre includes: *A Christmas Carol, A Midsummer Night's Dream, Snow White and Other Tales from the Brothers Grimm, Hamlet, Treasure Island, As You Like It, The Wind in the Willows* (Creation Theatre Company), *Twelfth Night* (Rose Theatre Bankside), *Catastrophic Sex Music* (Theatre 503 & Faster Pussycat Theatre Company, Denmark), *Top Girls, Dancing at Lughnasa, Absent Friends, Stockholm, The Rivals, Under Milkwood, King David Man of Blood, Julius Caesar, Road, The Resistible Rise of Arturo Ui, The Triumph of Love, Oh What a Lovely War, Present Laughter, Death of a Salesman, The Recruiting Officer* (Mercury Theatre, Colchester), *Eve Ryman* (European tour), *Absurd Person Singular* (Oldham Coliseum), *Oliver* (New Vic, Stoke), *Half a Sixpence* (West Yorkshire Playhouse*)*, *It's a Lovely Day Tomorrow, The Boy with a bomb in his Crisps, Cinderella, Sleeping Beauty, Jack and the Beanstalk* (Belgrade Theatre) and *Children in Uniform* (Battersea Arts Centre).

Film & Voice Over includes: *London Road* (National Theatre Flims), *Of Mice and Men* (Short night films), *JimJam & Sunny* (BBC), *Future Bright* (ITV).

ELEANOR JACKSON | Chloe

Eleanor trained at Bristol Old Vic Theatre School. Her work in theatre includes *Medea* at Bristol Old Vic, *Playhouse Creatures* at the Tobacco Factory, *Trojan Women* at the Bristol Old Vic Studio, *Songs for a New World* (NYMT) at the Bridewell and *The Hired Man* (NYMT) at Hull Truck Theatre. TV includes *Doctors*. She was also the runner-up for the Stephen Sondheim Student Performer of the Year award 2016.

CREATIVE TEAM

TONY CASEMENT | Director

Directing credits include: *Jump out of Skin* (Pleasance Theatre); *A Christmas Carol; The Rebel and the Run Away* (GLYPT); *Plague Days* (The Gravity Fields Festival); *John Simmonds* (The National Maritime Museum); *The Boy Who Followed His Dreams* (Unicorn); *Aladdin* (Blue Box Entertainment); *Hare and Tortoise; Saturday Night and Sunday Morning; Sleeping Beauty; Arsenic and Old Lace; The Grapes of Wrath; Much Ado About Nothing; Through the Leaves; Journey's End* (included in the Daily Telegraph's top ten productions of 2008); *The Promise*; and *The Angina Monologues* (Mercury Theatre); *Mary and the Midwives* (Eastern Angles); *The Vortex* (BSA); *Swimming* (Mercury, Cambridge, Soho Theatre); *Horizons; The Love Concept* (Frequency Theatre); *Little Angels* (Essex Playwriting Contest); *C U Next Tuesday* (The Town House Group); *Edward Gant's Amazing Feats of Loneliness* (Lakeside Theatre).

As adaptor and director: *The Changeling* (East15); *Tis Pity She's a Whore* (Lakeside Theatre); *Quadrophenia*, which he co – adapted from the album with Kenny Emson (The Mercury Theatre); *The Island* (East15); *Call of the Wild* (Greenwich Theatre).

As a writer his produced work includes: *For the Benefit of Capital* (East15); *Breaking the Jump* (a short film for Queen Mary's University); *Martha and Mary* (Mercury Theatre); *The Smithereens* (Mercury Theatre). *Aladdin* (Beckton Theatre), which he co-wrote with Neil Bromley and *A Pig Too Far* (BBC R4) and *Turn the World Down* (Channel 4), both of which he co-wrote with Neil Bromley and Iain Gonoude. *Turn the World Down* was nominated for a Golden Rose at the Montreux International Television Festival.

NICOLA WERENOWSKA | Writer

After a brief flirtation with playwriting when she was 16 (her first play "20%" was runner-up in the 1988 Royal Court Young Playwrights' Competition), Nicola began her playwriting journey by joining a local playwrights' group in 2003, following her life transforming diagnosis of dyspraxia. Productions include: *Davy's Day* (Mercury, 2004); *Peapickers* (Eastern Angles, 2007); *Freedoms of the Forest* (Menagerie, 2008); *Birth-Date* (Nabakov, 2012, part of 'Best Years' series); *CASH!* (Mercury, 2013); *Tu I Teraz* (Hampstead, The Nuffield, the Mercury, 2012/13); *Tattooed Under Your Skin* (Theatre 503, Acts of Defiance Festival, 2016); *HIDDEN* (Oxford Playhouse, Norwich Arts Centre, the Marlowe, the Mercury). Her work has been long-listed for national playwriting competitions including the Verity Bargate, the Bruntwood and Papa Tango. Nicola has been a writer on Graeae's attachment scheme, 'Write to Play', a member of the Royal Court National Writers' group and is playwright in residence at Essex University.

ANNA KELSEY | Set & Costume Designer

Anna trained at The Royal Welsh College of Music and Drama in Cardiff, graduating with a first class (BA) hons degree.

Theatre Includes: *Our Town* (The Watermill Theatre), *Under Milk Wood* (The Watermill Theatre), *Half the World Away* (Foursquare Theatre), *Macbeth, Spamalot, The Vicar of Dibley* (Cardiff Open Air Festival), *Women Power and Politics* (ALRA), *Moby Dick The Musical* (The Union Theatre), *Shirley Valentine* (The Lighthouse Theatre), *The Great American Trailer Park* (Waterloo East Theatre), *1001 Nights* (Queens Theatre, Hornchurch), *Theatre Clwyd @ Elfed* (Theatre Clwyd), *The Winters Tale* (RWCMD).

Assistant Designer: *Felini Book of Dreams* (Elan Frantoio), *Richard III* (Omidaze Theatre) *Caucasian Chalk Circle* (National Youth Theatre Wales). Anna was the recipient of the Prince of Wales Scholarship RWCMD 2014. She was also shortlisted for The Linbury Prize for Stage Design 2015.

VALERIE CHRISTIANSEN | Assistant Director

Valerie Christiansen is a Canadian performer and theatre director. She has directed a number of productions that involve community engagement including, *Pipef@%!* (Vancouver Fringe 2015), *Far To Close* (Art for Impact: Communities of Isolation and Alternative Creation Studios 2015), *Fit To Touch* (Popcorn Galaxies' New Narratives: an enviro-art extravaganza and Back Alley Artists Night @ CBC Studios- Vancouver, BC 2016) *Static Unheard Noises* (Vancouver Vines Art Festival 2016), *Wet Ink* (Vines Art Festival 2017.) She is currently an MFA directing student at East 15.

EASTERN ANGLES THEATRE COMPANY | Producer

Eastern Angles is the regional touring theatre company for East Anglia. It has a national reputation for producing high-quality, new writing with a regional flavour. Based at the Sir John Mills Theatre in Ipswich and The Undercroft in Peterborough, the company has been touring professional theatre productions into the towns and villages of East Anglia since 1982. Eastern Angles also stage productions in 'found spaces', like tithe barns, heritage sites and aircraft hangars, and have toured shows to The Soho and Bush Theatres and Edinburgh Festival Fringe. Future work includes a linked pair of productions featuring the Norfolk and Suffolk Broads and a large-scale project celebrating East region's rich, but often overlooked, contribution to theatre in the medieval era when "East Anglia was the West End of fifteenth century English Drama".

The regional touring company for the East of England

Artistic Director:	Ivan Cutting
Development / Communications Manager:	Karen Goddard
Administrator:	Jess Baker
Marketing Officer:	Helena Quarmby
Production Manager:	Steve Cooney
Stage Manager:	Penny Griffin
Theatre & Outreach Manager:	Jon Tavener
Finance:	Neil Hammond
Box Office:	Hazel Hicks
Peterborough Project Manager:	Keely Mills
Housekeeper:	Dot McDermott

Board of Trustees: Sue Arnold, Jayne Austin, Gill Brigg, Dr Peter Funnell (Chair), Hassina Khan, Laura Locke, Marilyn Martin, James Skellorn, Alison Stewart, Paul Winter

Ipswich Office:
Sir John Mills Theatre,
Gatacre Road,
Ipswich, IP1 2LQ

Peterborough Office:
Chauffeur's Cottage,
St Peter's Road,
Peterborough, PE1 1YX

Admin: 01473 218202 | **Box Office:** 01473 211498
admin@easternangles.co.uk | www.easternangles.co.uk

Twitter: @easternangles
Facebook: /EasternAnglesTheatreCompany
Instagram: @easternangles
#Guesthouse

To Margery Louvain Brice (née Joy) and Brenda De Ath

The Guest House

This being human is a guest house.
Every morning a new arrival.

A joy, a depression, a meanness,
some momentary awareness comes
as an unexpected visitor.

Welcome and entertain them all!
Even if they're a crowd of sorrows,
who violently sweep your house
empty of its furniture,
still, treat each guest honorably.
He may be clearing you out
for some new delight.

The dark thought, the shame, the malice.
meet them at the door laughing and invite them in.

Be grateful for whatever comes.
because each has been sent
as a guide from beyond.

Jelaluddin Rumi

ACKNOWLEDGEMENT AND THANKS

This production of 'Guesthouse' has been made possible by the generous support of the following organisations:

Eastern Angles Theatre Company, Grants For The Arts (East), the Mercury Theatre, Essex Book Festival, Vivacity, Ipswich Borough Council, Essex County Council, Suffolk County Council, Norfolk County Council, Babergh and Mid Suffolk Councils, Ipswich Building Society, Foyle Foundation, Lakeside Theatre, West Cliff Theatre, Menagerie Theatre Company, Firstsite.

Thanks to: Tony Casement, Ivan Cutting, Barbara Peirson, Paul George, Patrick Morris, Chris Howcroft, Christine Absalom, Jutta Austin, Amanda Haberland Jones, Alice Stacey, Matthew Linley, Patsy Humm, Richard and Violet Brice, Joanna Gentry, Angela Eyre, Luisa White, Alison Fogg, Daniel Buckroyd, Dan Sherer, Neil Jones, Norman Jacobs, Kerith Ririe, Belinda Farrell.

Special Thanks to: a wonderful cast and creative team and everyone at Eastern Angles.

CHARACTERS

VAL: 68, owner of a Clacton guesthouse

LISA: 41, Val's estranged daughter

CHLOE: 24, Lisa's daughter, brought up by Val

Action takes place in Clacton, 2017.

ACT 1.

1. MEMORY: BLUE LAGOON, 1963

Val is outside the Blue Lagoon watching the ballroom dancing.

VAL: It is 1963 and I am 13 years old and it is summer and I am outside the Blue Lagoon. (*beat*) I press my nose against the glass... the dancing is... the dancing is fantastic – fast and high, and the skirts are pink and the petticoats dance like the waves, and the music... I want to hear the music, (*beat*) I want to be inside. (*beat*) Dad says I'll be 16 soon enough but 3 summers is forever. (*beat*) Some boys are mucking about and out of nowhere Mrs K appears, 'Stop gawping and get a move on! Off you go!' Everyone is scared of Mrs K, even the grown-ups, you'd think she owned the world, not just the pier. Now the boys are sloping off. I step back too, away from the window, but I can't leave. I know it's dinner in a minute but I can't take my eyes away. (*pause*) The other kids aren't coming back and I get right close again. Inside they're jiving, and my feet are moving. (*she starts dancing*) Dad is teaching me to dance but he can't stand, so he shouts instructions, and he only knows the foxtrot and I want to rock and roll and I (*beat*) ...there's someone watching me, not holiday folk, Brian Joy, the boy from Golden Sands. He's two years above at school and I'm feeling hot and burning and I stop and he says, 'Nice try, kiddo'. And he's laughing like he knows everything about the world and I know nothing and I am not laughing back, I am pretending he's not there. (*beat*) But then he says, 'I'll show you one day, kiddo,' and I want to shout 'when?', but the words get stuck in my throat (*tries to say 'when'*), and he's gone. (*beat*) He's gone.

2. COLCHESTER HOSPITAL, SEPT 2017 (early pm)

Val is asleep in a chair. Lisa enters, anxious. Val stirs. They look at each other uncomfortably. Pause.

VAL: You...

LISA: How are you?

VAL: Alright.

LISA: I come as fast as I could. (*pause*) Yeah I got a call from the police. You didn't open the door to a guest, the light was on, they didn't know what to do... you was on the floor, mum, and they...

VAL: I know what happened.

LISA: Yeah, sorry I... I'm sorry.

VAL: For what?

LISA: (*pause*) All of it.

VAL: I'm thirsty.

LISA: There you go. (*passes Val water, Val drinks*)

VAL: More, please, love. (*Lisa pours her more water*) That's better.

LISA: You were in a coma, mum

VAL: Oh, don't be a drama queen, Lisa.

LISA: I didn't even know you had diabetes.

VAL: That's my private business.

LISA: Yeah but I...

VAL: (*interrupts*) And everyone's got diabetes these days. Sign of the times. I read it on the mail online. Too

	much sugar in processed food. You want to watch yourself.
LISA:	What…?
VAL:	You could do with an inch or two off that waistline. (*pause*) GP said it's lifestyle. I said, 'Do you know how many stairs I climb in a day?'
LISA:	You was unconscious.
VAL:	I'm alright. (*pause*)
LISA:	Mum…
VAL:	I'm waiting for Chloe.
LISA:	She's on the 1 o'clock. I phoned her last night.
VAL:	Do you phone her much?
LISA:	No.
VAL:	I'm only asking. She's your daughter. You're entitled to…
LISA:	(*interrupts*) I had to tell her. In case she didn't know. I'm next of kin, so they called me first and then I called her.
VAL:	Next of kin? (*laughing*) You make it sound like I'm dead.
LISA:	Don't! I… sorry… I… I couldn't park the car just now.
VAL:	You was always rubbish at parking.
LISA:	I couldn't do it.
VAL:	Lis?

LISA: There's no spaces and I'm driving round and round and...

VAL: (*interrupts*) Make you pay for the parking, do they?

LISA: Yeah. (*searching for painkillers*) Sorry I... I got a headache. (*Lisa takes painkillers*)

VAL: Now that's what I call criminal. Lucky I come in an ambulance.

LISA: Mum! Don't!

VAL: Well you live just round the corner. If I'd have got a cab from Clacton. (*she starts to get up, using crutches*)

LISA: Are you...?

VAL: You want to get a bus next time. (*beat*) Bathroom.

LISA: I'll help you. (*pause*) Let me help you. (*pause*) Your leg.

VAL: (*not looking at Lisa*) Not even broken.

LISA: You've got a bad sprain. The nurse...

VAL: (*interrupts*) Like I said, not even broken.

LISA: I want to help you, mum. (*beat*) I want to come back with you.

VAL: What?

LISA: To Golden Sands. To help you out.

VAL: You...?

LISA: Yeah.

VAL: I feel like I'm back in the coma.

LISA: They won't discharge you like this, not on your own.

VAL: Oh, are you a Dr now?

LISA: You won't manage all the stairs for one thing and…

VAL: (*interrupts*) Lisa when have I ever not managed? I had a bad day. Some locum whinging about the power shower in No 6, Hajar calls off sick, and then to top it all, I get a bad review. My eggs! How long I been cooking eggs?

LISA: I don't know.

VAL: But you know what a bad day is?

LISA: Yeah.

VAL: My sugar was low. I had a fall, and now I'm better. End of.

LISA: (*with difficulty*)Things change, mum.

VAL: I know how you feel about Clacton, love.

LISA: I heard it's alright now.

VAL: Alright?

LISA: What they're doing on the pier.

VAL: Oh yes, it's all done up lovely on the front. New owners, new rides. Have you come down for a peek?

LISA: No.

VAL: That's a shame! Would have done you the world of good. A stroll down the pier. A bit of fresh in your cheeks.

LISA: I'd have to come see you if I was down.

VAL: (*pause*) It's good for me, the pier. Good for business. People used to say, 'Bring back Butlins!', I'd say, let's start with the pier.

LISA: I would have come.

VAL: Let's not pretend, love.

LISA: I want to help.

VAL: Do you? Do you think the guests will want to be looking at your miserable mug? You got a keep a smile on. No matter what happens, how horrible it is, you got to keep smiling.

LISA: I will, I'll…

VAL: (*interrupts*) I don't need your help.

LISA: (*pause*) People change.

VAL: Do they?

LISA: You'll have to stop it one day. You can't go on forever.

VAL: It's my home. (*pause*) How dare you? Has your Markie put you up to this? Does he want me to sell up and get his hands on a share of the profits?

LISA: I don't think there'll…

VAL: (*interrupts*) Fancy a little retirement pad in Spain, does he?

LISA: He's got nothing to do with it.

VAL: Lisa, you have your life and I have mine, and now if you'll excuse me, I do need…

LISA: (*interrupts*) It hasn't got to be like this. (*Val exits, calling after her*) Mum! (*Lisa takes out cigarette packet* *as if desperate to smoke, massages her head, starts eating grapes she's brought for Val, Chloe enters with flowers and chocolates)* Chloe!

CHLOE: Where is she?

LISA: Bathroom.

CHLOE: Is she...?

LISA: She's alright.

CHLOE: Alright?

LISA: No, no, I mean not alright, she's had a bad knock and she... she looks... I don't know.

CHLOE: What?

LISA: I don't know. Pale and...

CHLOE: And what?

LISA: Like... smaller. *(beat)* She looks smaller. *(beat)* She'll be alright. *(pause)* The nurse says they'll discharge her this afternoon. She'll just need someone to keep an eye. Stop her sprinting up the stairs. *(pause)* She'll be so pleased you're here.

CHLOE: Of course I'm here. Did you think I wouldn't... do you know how worried I've been? I haven't slept.

LISA: Nor me.

CHLOE: I can see that.

LISA: She's my mum, Chloe.

CHLOE: Who you never visit. You live 16 miles away and you never visit.

LISA: You know how it is...

CHLOE: (*speaking over her*) You don't even drop in on her to see how she is.

LISA: I want to change that.

CHLOE: Since when?

LISA: I don't know. Ages. I don't...

CHLOE: (*speaking over her*) You're only here now because you live here.

LISA: She don't want to see me.

CHLOE: That's not true. You're the one who...

(*Val returns, the women stop arguing, look at one another*)

CHLOE: Mummy Val!

VAL: Chloe. (*they hug one another*)

CHLOE: MV, how are you? I am... I am so relieved to see you. How are you?

VAL: Not so bad.

CHLOE: Here, let me... (*she helps Val back to chair*)

VAL: Now I don't like you missing work.

CHLOE: It's fine.

VAL: What, you get back to London and you got to race straight back again?

CHLOE: Actually I've taken the week off. (*pause*) I'm coming back with you.

LISA: I said I would...

CHLOE: (*to Val*) And I insist.

VAL: Do I look like an invalid?

LISA: I'm local, so it makes sense...

CHLOE: (*to Val*) You said you wanted to see more of me?

VAL: Yes, to come and visit, not to move in, you've got your life there.

CHLOE: Just a week. To help you back on your feet.

VAL: How about your fella?

CHLOE: He insisted.

VAL: (*pause*) Alright.

CHLOE: Fantastic! I've got myself a holiday!

VAL: It won't be a holiday, sweetheart.

LISA: I've got the car. I can drive you back. When you're discharged.

VAL: I hope it's soon.

CHLOE: (*to Lisa*) We'll get a cab.

LISA: To Clacton?

VAL: I got three guests to check in.

CHLOE: (*to Lisa*) I got it covered.

LISA: (*to Chloe*) That's mad, you'll be looking at fifty quid when I'm here with the car and...

CHLOE: (*interrupts*) Save you hanging around. It could be ages before the doctor gets to us.

VAL: I hope not. How about check in? Could you do it, Chloe?

CHLOE: Of course.

LISA: Just let me drive you back, mum. (*pause*)

VAL: You'll be wanting to get back to your school, Lis.

LISA: No, I don't.

VAL: Fed up with it, are you?

LISA: No.

VAL: (*to Chloe*) She only wants me to sell up.

CHLOE: Sell up...?

VAL: The house!

CHLOE: Sell Golden Sands?

LISA: No, I... I...

CHLOE: (*interrupts, to Lisa*) Don't you know what it means to her?

LISA: Look, what I said was...

CHLOE: (*interrupts*) It's her life.

LISA: I know. I do know that.

CHLOE: And you want to take it from her!

LISA: With her health... well, everyone gets older and...

VAL: She wants me out!

LISA: No...

VAL: Be ordering my coffin next!

CHLOE: MV!

LISA: No.

VAL: And I'm not retiring.

CHLOE: Of course not. When you need it, if you need it... I'll pay for extra staff.

VAL: Chloe!

CHLOE: When and if you need it.

VAL: I'm alright.

LISA: You can't go on forever, Mum. No one can.

CHLOE: (*to Lisa*) I'll move in with her.

VAL: Move in...?

CHLOE: If it comes to it, why not?

VAL: You've got a life in London, sweetheart.

CHLOE: (*to Lisa*) It's about priorities.

VAL: Yes and I've check in to worry about. Now that's my priority.

CHLOE: Don't worry, MV, I'll do it.

VAL: You're a godsend. That's what you are. A treasure.

CHLOE: MV! (*beat*) Now, why don't we find out when you are getting discharged?

LISA: We got to wait for...

CHLOE: (*Speaking over her*) I'll try and speak to someone.

VAL: Don't you want a cup of tea first?

CHLOE: I want to get you home. I'll be two minutes. (*exits*)

(*Pause*)

LISA: Do you want a cup of tea, mum?

VAL: I'm alright. (*pause*) You get one for Chloe. Oh and a sandwich. I do worry about that girl, dashing about like a mad thing. (*Gets out money from purse*)

LISA: I'll get it.

VAL: There's a place round the corner, I think.

LISA: (*Lisa hesitates*) Mum…

VAL: Lis?

LISA: I don't know what she likes.

VAL: What?

LISA: The sandwich. I don't know what she likes.

VAL: Well, she's not fussy. She's not keen on tuna and I wouldn't trust egg mayo in a place like this. I don't think BLT's her thing.

LISA: Right.

VAL: Oh and avoid mustard.

LISA: Yeah. (*Lisa moves to ext, stops suddenly, overwhelmed. Val sighs, exits*)

3. MEMORY: COLCHESTER, 2010

*Chloe is at a 6*th *form open evening with Val. Lisa is waiting for her in the car.*

LISA: It's 2017. (*beat*) It's 2010. She's at the sixth form college evening. In Colchester, and I'm waiting. I picked 'em up from North station and dropped 'em up the Hill. You can park here in the evenings. It's not too bad. (*beat*) I could go home. (*beat*) I don't… it's alright waiting, safe in the car. Mark said, 'Why don't you drive down to Golden Sands and get 'em? Save them the train.' (*beat*) If I thought mum would say yes. (*beat*) Then he goes, 'Why don't you invite Chloe to stay over? She's big enough, she can decide.' (*laughs*) He means well. Sees me like this, wants to help. He feels bad about… he can't say it, he don't have to say it. (*beat*) Once he said we should go down the IVF route maybe, maybe that would make me happy. God my throat went dry, when he… it's dry now. Got some pastilles somewhere. (*beat*) Like I can replace her with some bloody test tube freak. (*beat*) I don't want to hurt him. (*pause*)

I can see them coming now, Chloe's smiling, excited, getting in the car with mum. I want to know how it went, 'Was it alright?' 'You can learn here', she says and she's squeezing Mum's hand and yeah… (*beat*) So I'm pulling away, giving it some gas down the hill cos MV don't want to miss the 9 o'clock. 'It's like I'm leaving Clacton behind,' Chloe says as she gets out of the car. And I want to tell her that you never leave a place because it's in here. (*pause*) I wait for them at the station, watch 'em come up the stairs onto the platform. (*pause*) When Mark comes in from football, I'm sitting in the dark. I don't forget to switch the lights on, it don't matter.

4. GUESTHOUSE, SEPT 2017, (a week after Scene 2, am)

Chloe mopping up water in a guest's room. Val is calling for her from downstairs.

VAL: Chloe..? Chloe?

CHLOE: I'm up here.

VAL: Up top?

CHLOE: Yeah.

VAL: Can you clear up breakfast, sweetheart?

CHLOE: No.

VAL: Chloe? What's going on?

CHLOE: I'm busy.

VAL: I need you down here. Chloe? Chloe? (*enters on crutches*) That old shower.

CHLOE: Yeah.

VAL: Always a pain in the backside this one.

CHLOE: It's going to go through the floorboards.

VAL: Yes, I've called Reggie.

CHLOE: Who?

VAL: The plumber. You remember him? He used to live down Thornbury Road, then he…

CHLOE: (*interrupts*) I don't care where he lives! Where is he?

VAL: He's always busy. He's very good, you see.

CHLOE: Did you tell him it's an emergency?

VAL: It's not an emergency!

CHLOE: Yes it is!

VAL: Chloe!

CHLOE: Sorry! I... sorry.

VAL: The locum's next door. Dr Singh. He's a regular.

CHLOE: I said I'm sorry. It's just... this.

VAL: It's an old building, sweetheart.

CHLOE: It's a mess.

VAL: There's always a leak somewhere.

CHLOE: Yes but I thought you got this one fixed. When I got here last week, and that lady complained.

VAL: She was the complaining sort.

CHLOE: MV, what do you expect? Look, you called the plumber, yes?

VAL: Yes, Reggie came and had a look.

CHLOE: So why...?

VAL: Oh it was a temporary fix. It's on its last legs this unit. And the one in number 2. He wanted a grand to do a whole lot of plumbing Can you believe that?

CHLOE: That sounds reasonable for...

VAL: Well, yes, if and when the money comes in.

CHLOE: The money is in.

VAL: Have you seen the books recently?

CHLOE: We've been full house nearly every night since...

VAL: (*interrupts*) Yes, the conference. You get your busy times and...

CHLOE: (*interrupts*) MV, the plumber...

VAL: (*interrupts*) Reggie

CHLOE: ...he needs to come back now and sort it out.

VAL: Give him a chance!

CHLOE: I'll call him. What's the number?

VAL: Sweetheart, calm down. Alright.

CHLOE: It's a mess.

VAL: You're not yourself at all.

CHLOE: A total mess!

VAL: Tell you what, I'll finish breakfasts and you can have a little breather. Give yourself ten minutes in quarters and have a hot chocolate.

CHLOE: I don't drink hot chocolate.

VAL: You used to! With marshmallows and cream.

CHLOE: MV!

VAL: You've been a good girl, Chloe. Getting up early, getting stuck in with me...you're not used to it. You don't even clean your fella's pad.

CHLOE: The cleaner was there before I moved in.

VAL: So you got out of the habit. I'm not complaining. People do things different these days. In London.

CHLOE: Look, I'm sorry I forgot to finish that room the other day, but...

VAL: (*interrupts*) I blamed Hajar to start with. I had to give the guest a 20% discount in the end.

CHLOE: You called me to sort out the conference booking while I was in the middle of cleaning the room and then...

VAL: You want to cut down on the booze, sweetheart.

CHLOE: No, I want to increase it.

VAL: That's your trouble. You stay up late, Skyping your fella, drinking wine.

CHLOE: A glass or two.

VAL: Not good when you're up at 5.

CHLOE: MV, this... it's not about me. It's about you.

VAL: Me? I'm alright.

CHLOE: No, you're not.

VAL: Well, I done my leg in, but it's healing nicely.

CHLOE: It's not about your leg. This week, seeing you struggle with everything...

VAL: Once I get up and running again. Like you was saying, we've been nearly full house out of season.

CHLOE: Yes, but... this place... it's falling to bits, MV. It's too much for you. Keeping up with everything. Look at that double booking.

VAL: Everyone makes mistakes sometimes.

CHLOE: The bathroom leaking, the linen, marketing the special functions – you can't manage on your own. No one could. You know, it's crazy you doing this for all this time with almost no staff, and I'm going back today.

VAL: Today?

CHLOE: Yeah. It's been a week.

VAL: Just slipped my mind for a minute. (*pause*)

CHLOE: Is your sugar ok?

VAL: A week goes quickly.

CHLOE: Yeah. (*pause*) You know I'd love to stay longer.

VAL: Would you?

CHLOE: Of course, but I've...

VAL: Would you? (*pause*) Stay on a bit, sweetheart. I don't know what I'd have done without you when we got back from the hospital. And I got two funeral parties next week. I do a good funeral tea. I could give you a few tips for mine.

CHLOE: MV!

VAL: I'm joking!

CHLOE: You need to hire more staff.

VAL: If I could afford it.

CHLOE: You can!

VAL: I don't think so.

CHLOE: Ok, I'll pay. For more staff.

VAL: What?

CHLOE: That's the obvious solution. I'll pay for someone to help you out and then we can start to sort out what needs sorting.

VAL: And how are you going to that? You're a secretary.

CHLOE: Administrator.

VAL: I know the price of London rents.

CHLOE: I don't pay any rent.

VAL: Don't you?

CHLOE: The mortgage, it's in Tom's name and he's been paying it on his own for four years before...

VAL: (*interrupts*) I didn't think that's how you did it these days.

CHLOE: He earns stacks, MV.

VAL: And you've been brought up to pay your way.

CHLOE: And to be careful. I'm saving up.

VAL: For your dance company?

CHLOE: (*hesitates*) Yeah.

VAL: Well, that's something. (*beat*) Just a few more days, sweetheart. Would you? Another week I'll be fully recovered. You heard the physio, I'm lucky to have got off...

CHLOE: (*interrupts*) I have to get back.

VAL: You're missing your fella?

CHLOE: MV, my job.

VAL: Please. Chloe. Please. (*pause*) If you go, I... psychologically... it's taken it out of me.

CHLOE: MV, I just offered to pay for...

VAL: (*interrupts*) I like you being around.

CHLOE: (*pause*) I'll come back soon.

VAL: When you're around, this place, it's lighter. (*beat*) Sometimes I get... empty. Makes me chuckle. All these guests, toing and froing, asking for this, that and the other and I...

CHLOE: (*interrupts*) I think you should sell up.

VAL: What?

CHLOE: I think it's time.

VAL: You been talking to Lisa?

CHLOE: No.

VAL: Discussing me behind my back?

CHLOE: Of course not.

VAL: Are you sure?

CHLOE: I never talk to her. You know I never talk to her.

VAL: (*interrupts*) She wants the profits from this place.

CHLOE: I don't.

VAL: Don't you?

CHLOE: No. MV, how could you even say that?

VAL: You've changed your tune.

CHLOE: This place... It's making you ill. And I don't want to see you ill.

(*pause*)

VAL: I thought you was on my side.

CHLOE: I am. (*pause*) Mummy Val?

VAL: You said you'd move in with me.

CHLOE: I... yeah... I...

VAL: (*interrupts*)At the hospital. That's what you said.

CHLOE: I know I said it...

VAL: (*interrupts*) But you didn't mean it?

CHLOE: Yes, no. Yes. In the moment, I meant it in the moment.

VAL: You didn't mean it.

CHLOE: MV. (*bell rings*) Not now, shall I...?

VAL: (*interrupts*) I'll do it. You want to get back to your job.

CHLOE: Don't be... You wanted me to be in London, right. That's what you've always wanted for me.

VAL: I want you to be in London but I want you back here, only I don't because I want you in London, but you can't be in two places at once. You're only ever where you are.

CHLOE: Yeah.

VAL: I wanted you to have a good life. A future. The dancing classes. All those shows and competitions. I made sacrifices for you.

CHLOE: But now you make it sound like I'm selfish because I can't suddenly drop everything.

VAL: I wanted things once, Chloe.

CHLOE: What...?

VAL: For me. (*pause*) A life... a different life. I could have gone to university.

CHLOE: But you chose Golden Sands...

VAL: (*beat*) I loved your Grandad.

CHLOE: Yeah...

VAL: I made my choice. (*beat*) I talk to him sometimes, ask his advice. 'What would you do, Bri?' (*beat*) What, do you think I'm having another hypo?

CHLOE: No.

VAL: Or Alzheimers?

CHLOE: Grandad, what do you think he'd say? About all this?

VAL: Get Lisa round to help, that's what he'd say.

CHLOE: Really...?

VAL: No doubt at all. I've told you what he was like. Spoiled her rotten. Give her anything. Forgive her anything. (*beat*) He didn't see her grow up.

CHLOE: MV, you need someone, some help, I don't know, extra staff or... Lisa, but you...

VAL: I need you.

CHLOE: And I have to go back.

VAL: (*pause*) If that's what you choose.

CHLOE: I'm doing everything I can to help. I don't know...

VAL: (*speaking over her*) It was a little thing, the fall.

CHLOE: MV, are you...? (*bell rings*) Damn it, shall I...?

VAL: Sometimes a little thing... it... turns things inside out in your head. Like everything shifts and you don't know what to think. (*bell rings again*)

CHLOE: I'll go. (*moves to exit*)

VAL: No one goes on forever.

(*Val looks around the room as if seeing it for the first time. Pause. She checks her sugar, takes Insulin pen from fridge. Injects.*)

5. MEMORY: THE BRIDGE, 1966.

Val is standing on the Venetian bridge eating an ice cream.

VAL: It is 2017. It is 1966. I am sixteen years old and I am on the Venetian bridge with Brian Joy from the Golden Sands Guesthouse and he has bought me a 99 and I am on top of the world. (*whispers*) Now I am 16, I know what boys want and why you mustn't give it to them. (*beat*) And we are not courting regular but sometimes he waits for me after school and we go down the pier and he says he'll take me to Cordys for tea when his Mum pays him for helping out with changeover. (*beat*) I've never been to Cordys before. It's where the holiday folk go mostly, you see them queuing outside. (*pause*)

Sandra says Brian is trouble because her mum says his Dad is a ladies' man and he'll never stick with me and his mum is posh and don't like Jaywick folk. I say, 'You're jealous,' and she says, 'You'll never be good enough for Brian Joy and that's a fact!' and I say, 'Why?' and she says, 'because you can't dance.' (*beat*) She's right. Brian is an ace dancer, and I've two left feet. (*beat*) His pals call him a sissy but then he does a bit of singing outside the West Cliff Theatre and people stop and listen. (*beat*) Then the boys shut up. (*beat*) Brian wants to be on the stage. That is his secret, and I know it. He asked me mine – my secret – and I said, (*beat*) 'I want to go to university.' I hadn't said it before, I hadn't thought it before but I'm doing A levels now and I like it, I like English best, and Dad says I got a good brain but Mum says I'm lazy because I got my head in a book half the time. (*beat*) I tell her it's exciting, diving into other people's worlds and… she don't get it. But she can't stop me reading, no one can. (*beat*) But you can't live off other people's stories all your life, you got to live your own.

6. GUESTHOUSE, quarters, NOV 2017, (early pm)

Quarters seems less cluttered, tidier, flowers on table. Val is researching holiday destinations online, eating a bowl of soup. Lisa enters with a large pile of sheets.

VAL: (*not looking up*) That lot in No 8 still hanging about, love?

LISA: I checked them out. They liked the new menu.

VAL: You're a smart girl.

LISA: What about these?

VAL: (*looking up*) My spares? What are you doing with them?

LISA: Sorting out the linen room.

VAL: Everyone needs spares.

LISA: These have got to go, mum.

VAL: (*picks up sheet, examines it, puts it to her face, beat*) Well, yes. I suppose they've seen better days.

LISA: And we need new towels.

VAL: What's wrong with my towels? I only got a new batch in last year.

LISA: If we're marketing high end, we need to be high end.

VAL: I don't want to be spending out on towels.

LISA: Sometimes you got to spend a bit before…

VAL: (*interrupts*) Not now, love. No. (*pause*) I'm thinking about a holiday.

LISA: A holiday?

VAL: Yes. You keep saying I should be kind to myself, don't you? And when was I last on holiday? (*pause*) Devon. I think. That's right. With Chloe. (*beat*) You didn't come.

LISA: I don't remember you going.

VAL: No, you was...

LISA: ...in that place?

VAL: (*slowly*) No. I think you was out of there. (*beat*) In the flats. You was in the flats. (*beat*) It rained all week, in Torquay. Chloe said she preferred it here. There's more to do indoors, she said. (*beat*) I fancy going abroad.

LISA: On your own?

VAL: Well, who's going to come with me?

LISA: I could... if you wanted...

VAL: You'll be looking after here, love. If you can get more time off, I don't know how much holiday...

LISA: (*interrupts*) I could...

VAL: (*speaking over her*) And if not, I always shut down in Feb for a week or so, so I'd...

LISA: (*interrupts*) I could get the time off.

VAL: (*pause*) Well, that's settled then. I just need to decide where I'm going. (*beat*) I went to Spain with your Dad.

LISA: Yeah.

VAL: Somewhere up by Malaga. We wanted to check out the package holiday, the hotel wasn't even built!

(*laughs*) Bri got frazzled like a tomato and I got a dicky tummy from the fish. (*pause*) I think I'll go for Italy. I like the sound of Venice or maybe... (*Val's mobile rings*) Oh where is the bugger? That might be Chloe. (*finds phone, disappointed it's not Chloe*) Yes, speaking, good morning. (*pause, to Lisa*) Excuse me, love. (*Val moves to one side, takes and ends call*)

LISA: Who was...?

VAL: (*quickly*) No one.

LISA: Alright. I only...

VAL: (*interrupts*) I was hoping it'd be Chloe.

LISA: Did she get back to you?

VAL: I only called her yesterday.

LISA: Yeah I meant last week. You called her...

VAL: (*interrupts*) She's very busy, Lisa. (*pause*)

LISA: I could call her.

VAL: Whatever for?

LISA: If I said you was wanting to talk to her...

VAL: (*interrupts*) She'll come when she's ready.

LISA: I'd like to talk to her.

VAL: Well, give her a call. You don't need my permission. (*beat*) Have you been to Rome?

LISA: No. (*beat*) I wouldn't know what to say.

VAL: Venice is still pushing my buttons.

LISA: I'd like to know what to say. (*pause, Val finishes soup*) Was it alright?

VAL: Lovely. (*beat*) You overdid it on the coriander, but not bad.

LISA: I followed the recipe.

VAL: I'm not criticising. You're a good cook. You've got your Dad's touch. He had an instinct for it. Sometimes that's what you need. You've got to feel your way around the ingredients.

LISA: I can't feel much at the minute. I can't taste. The sertraline. It does stuff to my taste buds.

VAL: All pills have side-effects.

LISA: I've upped the dosage.

VAL: Whatever keeps you on the straight and narrow.

LISA: I don't want to be on the straight and narrow.

VAL: Lisa...?

LISA: I want to feel. (*beat*) Sorry. (*beat*) I've had to give up my job.

VAL: What at St Beas's? (*pause*) I thought you was going back next week? What's happened? (*pause*) I thought you was happy there.

LISA: I like the kids.

VAL: So is it your boss?

LISA: No, no, she's... nice. (*beat*) It's Mark.

VAL: What doesn't he like you working in the same place no more? Seeing what he gets up to?

LISA: That's kind of it.

VAL: Kind of...?

LISA: Mark, he... he's got... there's someone. Someone else.

VAL: He's been cheating on you?

LISA: (*Lisa nods*)

VAL: Well, I... I don't know what to say, love. He doesn't seem the type. All tongue tied and non-stop rambling about socialist politics, calling UKIP a bunch of hooligans.

LISA: I don't blame him.

VAL: Well, I do!

LISA: You just don't like him.

VAL: I've got nothing against him. I was pleased when he took you on.

LISA: Took me on?

VAL: With all your troubles... I was relieved.

LISA: That I was out of your way?

VAL: Lisa! I only wanted you to be happy. Same as what everyone wants for their kids. (*pause*) So who is she?

LISA: A lab technician. In his department.

VAL: And what does she see in him? It can't be the conversation. Was she a mate of yours? Now that is mean, to...

LISA: (*interrupts*) I didn't know her.

VAL: The way people behave these days.

LISA: It's alright, mum. I'm alright with it. (*beat*) I don't want to work there no more.

VAL: Well, I'm not surprised. Are you divorcing him?

LISA: Yeah.

VAL: So you want to make sure he provides for you properly, don't let him get away with it. Squeeze what you can out of him.

LISA: It's not like that. (*pause*) Sometimes I had nothing to say to him. For days, weeks. (*pause*) When he told me he was seeing Helena, part of me was shocked that he'd cheated, but another part was thinking, why didn't he do it years ago? (*pause*)

VAL: And what happens now? How about your house?

LISA: He's moved out, for now. (*pause*) But I want to be here. (*pause*)

VAL: (*takes Lisa's hands.*) I could murder him.

LISA: Mum...

VAL: You're my daughter.

LISA: I'd like to move in, I mean like live here and work here, with you.

VAL: Don't you want to find another school?

LISA: Not really. And you need someone to...

VAL: ...To run the show?

LISA: Yeah. (*quickly*) I mean to do it with you. With you in charge. I can learn stuff from you.

VAL: You've got nothing to learn. You grew up here.

LISA: Are you saying...?

VAL: (*interrupts*) I don't know. (*beat*) I don't know. (*pause*) This... you and Markie, it's something of a shock. I need to have a think. I don't want you chucking in your career to run this place and then finding out it's not what you're after.

LISA: I'm only a classroom assistant.

VAL: You've got a profession.

LISA: We could see how it goes. Me staying here. While you think about it.

VAL: I'm not making any promises.

LISA: Thanks.

VAL: You're a good girl, Lisa. (*beat*) You both are. You and Chloe. (*beat*) And she'll be here soon. Seven weeks. I'm counting down on the calendar. We'll do something nice when she's here.

LISA: I don't know if she'll want me...

VAL: (*interrupts*) All three of us.

LISA: Mum...

VAL: I'm sorry about Markie.

LISA: It's over. (*beat*) I want it to be over.

7. MEMORY: MARTELLO BEACH, 1968

Val is sitting on the beach.

VAL: It is 2017. It is 1968 and I am eighteen years old and the envelope is burning in my hands. And I don't want to open it and I do at the same time. (*opens envelope*) And I'm smiling, I can't stop smiling because I've passed, I've passed everything. (*beat*) And on the beach, everyone else is smiling too because they're on holiday and the sun's out and there's Punch and Judy but... it's like they're smiling at me.

I could go. To teacher training college. I could be a teacher. If I wanted. I'm looking at the kids building sandcastles and I'm thinking I could make their lives matter. (*beat*) My brother, Kenny, he's going to be an engineer and work in an office and wear a suit. If you're a boy you can do that, college and what you want. If you're a girl... (*pause*)

Bri's asked me to marry him. Says he'll take me to Upchurches in Colchester to get the ring. And his mum likes me. She says I'm a sensible girl and with his Dad gone... it'll be ours one day. Golden Sands. One day we'll be running a guesthouse, me and Bri, and it's a good living, a good life, as long as you're clean and not too pricey and not mean on toast. And Bri'll do building on the side and we'll be quids in. (*pause*) I say to Bri, 'but what about your dancing?' (*beat*) He says he'll do cabaret for the guests and... he says no one can stop you dreaming and... one day... one day who knows what will happen? (*beat*) But he's got responsibilities now, he says, someone's got to help his mum. I look at him and I think he's grown up now and I... I feel like a kid. (*pause*)

It's so hot today, the town's like sardines. In the papers they're saying some people are going on planes to Spain for their holidays but you woldn't know it here. You'd think this place was the centre of the universe.

(*laughs, pause, looks at letter*) Bri says I can still go, to university. He'll wait... But when will I see him? And what about Golden Sands? And mum says he'll change his mind because men don't like brainy wives and I should know which side my bread is buttered. (*beat*) If I'd have failed, I wouldn't have a choice. (*beat*) But I wouldn't have made Dad proud.

8. GUESTHOUSE, quarters, DEC 2017, (early eve)

Val is decorating Christmas tree. Boxes of Xmas decorations everywhere. She gets frustrated. Stops, starts dancing. Chloe and Lisa enter.

VAL: Chloe?

CHLOE: Hello, MV.

VAL: Let's take a look at you! Come here, (*moves to hug Chloe, trips over box*) Ow!

LISA: Careful, mum!

CHLOE: Have you been at the sherry, MV?

VAL: No, I have not! I've been on my feet all day. But I am getting in a pickle with these decs. Look at it. All tangled up. You're going have to take over, Lis.

LISA: I thought we was going to do it together?

VAL: Yes, I got itchy feet. I wanted it to be all nice for Chloe. (*to Chloe*) How are you, sweetheart?

CHLOE: I'm… yeah, alright.

LISA: We always do it at night.

VAL: (*to Chloe*) Journey good?

CHLOE: Same old.

LISA: When it's dark.

VAL: (*to Chloe*) Lis thought you'd appreciate a lift back.

CHLOE: (*to Lisa*) Thanks.

LISA: You're welcome.

VAL: With all your luggage and whatnot.

LISA: Yeah, she's got a tonne.

VAL: (*to Chloe*) Bought back half of Selfridges for me?

CHLOE: Not exactly.

VAL: Harrods?

CHLOE: Sorry, MV.

VAL: That'll be next year then.

LISA: We got to sort this out.

VAL: Yes, we've been waiting for you, sweetheart.

CHLOE: I do it every year.

VAL: We can all dip in. She's very good at the tree, Lis.

LISA: Great.

VAL: Very artistic.

CHLOE: I'm not artistic…

VAL: Unlike me!

CHLOE: …I just do it. (*to Lisa*) And you're not here and…

LISA: (*interrupts*) I'm here now.

CHLOE: Yeah.

LISA: I was meaning you know…in the past.

VAL: Why don't you get Chloe's bags in, Lis?

LISA: I done it. They're in quarters.

VAL: Well, you're on top of things. Wish I could say the same. Now come and sit down, girls. We'll sort the tree later.

CHLOE: I want to find the angel.

VAL: Come on, have a sherry first. (*hands out drinks*) Cheers everyone.

LISA / CHLOE: Cheers!

VAL: (*to Chloe*) Now how are you really doing?

CHLOE: Yeah, you know.

VAL: You don't look too bad, I must say.

CHLOE: Thanks.

VAL: I mean considering he dumped you.

CHLOE: He didn't dump me.

VAL: Well, I'm sure it's for the best.

LISA: Yeah, I'm sorry, Chloe.

CHLOE: For what?

LISA: Your bloke.

CHLOE: It's fine.

VAL: At his posh folks' place now, is he?

CHLOE: I don't know where he is.

VAL: Let's hope he chokes on his turkey.

CHLOE: He's a vegetarian.

VAL: He never is?

CHLOE: Does it matter?

VAL: Well I'm glad you got rid of him.

LISA: Mum, it's personal...

VAL: (*interrupts*) I can't be doing with fussy eaters.

CHLOE: Can we stop talking about this!

VAL: Yes, let's have another drink. Nice spot of sherry this. (*beat*) Lisa?

LISA: No thanks.

VAL: You can let yourself have a small one.

LISA: We've still got guests to check in.

CHLOE: Really?

LISA: I put them in Number Seven.

CHLOE: (*to Val*) I'll drink hers.

VAL: (*to Chloe*) Don't overdo it, love.

CHLOE: Hello – it's Christmas, MV. (*Val and Chloe toast glasses*)

VAL: And we're busy!

CHLOE: Is Clacton finally on the up?

VAL: Like I been saying.

LISA: We've only got four checked in.

VAL: (*to Chloe*) Lisa's got a Christmas package on the go.

CHLOE: A what?

VAL: Yes, she's giving them a bit of a discount, and throwing in some mince pies and mulled wine. And it seems to be working.

LISA: It's early days.

VAL: And we're bigging up the lights. What do you think, Chloe?

CHLOE: I think this is Clacton and not bloody Lapland.

VAL: Chloe!

CHLOE: Just a joke!

VAL: And what are you doing, digging in that box?

CHLOE: Looking for Granddad's angel!

LISA: Do you mean that white thing?

VAL: Angels are normally white, Lis.

LISA: Like made out of an old toilet roll?

CHLOE: Can't you remember? Grandad made it for you.

LISA: No he never.

VAL: That's what we used to say. The angel was sent from Bri in heaven.

CHLOE: And he made it for Lisa when she was little.

LISA: He never made me no angel.

VAL: We used to pretend.

CHLOE: Pretend?

VAL: You liked it if I told the story that way.

CHLOE: So... where it is.

LISA: It was... yeah... damaged.

CHLOE: My angel!

LISA: Lots of the decs, you know… they'd had it, and… I chucked a load out.

CHLOE: You threw away Grandad's angel?

LISA: I… I don't know.

CHLOE: Did you throw it away or not?

LISA: I'm sorry.

VAL: Well, never mind. It was…

CHLOE: Never mind!

VAL: Lisa's been doing a bit of a spring clean while she's here.

CHLOE: (*to Lisa*) Why are you here?

VAL: Chloe!

LISA: You know why. Helping Mum out.

CHLOE: Yeah, because it suits you.

LISA: What?

CHLOE: Mark chucks you out, you've got nowhere to go, and…

LISA: (*interrupts*) No.

CHLOE: And now suddenly here you are, dictating when the tree gets done like you own the place.

LISA: I did it before you was born. (*pause*)

CHLOE: Can I have a top up?

VAL: Help yourself.

CHLOE: (*hesitates, drinks another glass quickly*) I'm not going back to London.

VAL: What do you mean?

CHLOE: I'm staying here with you.

VAL: Staying 'til when?

CHLOE: Not when! For good. I'm moving in, moving back. I'm coming home, MV.

VAL: I think you've had enough of that.

CHLOE: I know the last time I was here... but I've been thinking and...

VAL: (*interrupts*) Your job! What about your job?

CHLOE: (*grimacing*) The job, the job! The job bores me.

VAL: Have you given it up?

CHLOE: Not yet. (*beat*) I only decided on the train.

VAL: You haven't thought this through, love.

CHLOE: There are some things you don't need to think through. They just come at you in a moment and you know... you know what you need to do. (*beat*) The train stops suddenly at Thorpe and I'm thinking, 'God, we're so close', and then I look out of the window. There's this light and it's not snowing but it could. (*beat*) I realise I don't have to go back.

LISA: Chloe, the thing is...

VAL: (*speaking over Lisa*) Chloe, I know you're upset about your fella? What's his name? Tommie.

CHLOE: Tom! (*beat*) It's not about him.

VAL: Yes it is. I thought he was the one.

CHLOE: So did I. (*pause*) In the end it wasn't enough. (*pause*) Not like you and granddad.

VAL: No.

CHLOE: He proposed. I was going to say something like, 'I'm not ready' or 'Can we review this in six months time?' But that would have been lying.

VAL: Oh sweetheart.

CHLOE: So it all works out. I'm back home. It's perfect. It's the perfect solution.

LISA: I'm going to be managing here.

VAL: Lisa…?

LISA: I just want to get it straight.

CHLOE: You're going to live here?

VAL: (*to Lisa*) Well, I never said yes, love, we haven't…

LISA: (*interrupts*) No, but that's what you…

CHLOE: (*speaking over her*) You'll have to make other plans.

LISA: This is my plan.

CHLOE: MV, can you tell her that she'll have to rethink her plans.

LISA: I'm sure we can sort something out but…

CHLOE: (*interrupts*) There's nothing to sort. I'm back now.

VAL: Girls… listen…

LISA: (*to Chloe*) We could do it together.

CHLOE: Together!

LISA: Why not?

VAL: Girls! Please! Listen... listen... (*hesitates*)

LISA: Mum, your sugar...?

VAL: (*interrupts*) I'm alright.

CHLOE: Do you want a mince pie?

VAL: The house... I'm... I'm taking your advice.

CHLOE: (*to Lisa*) What have you said to her?

LISA: Nothing.

VAL: From the both of you.

LISA: Mum, are you sure you're...

CHLOE: (*speaking over her*) MV, last time I was here you begged me to stay and I let you down and I'm sorry but I'm here now.

LISA: Am I invisible here?

CHLOE: You've been invisible all my life.

LISA: No, no. I'm not having that, no.

VAL: (*pause*) The house is on the market.

CHLOE: What...?

LISA: We should check her sugar.

VAL: This is not about my diabetes. (*beat*) I'm selling up.

LISA: No. Why didn't you say? You said you'd think about it, about me running this place.

VAL: I have.

LISA: These last few weeks, months, I've put so much work in here, I...

VAL: And you done a good job.

LISA: I want to run this place.

VAL: No, you don't, you couldn't run anything. Things get tough and you run in the opposite direction...

LISA: (*interrupts, to Val*) And what are you doing that's so different?

CHLOE: (*to Lisa*) No one's cheated on her. You know, I don't blame Mark for...

VAL: (*interrupts*) Chloe! That's enough. (*beat*)

LISA: I could make it work, mum. You know I could. Get more people in, sort out the house.

VAL: My mind's made up.

CHLOE: MV, don't you want me back?

VAL: It's not what you want, sweetheart, not really.

CHLOE: Yes it is!

VAL: There's something else for you out there.

CHLOE: What?

VAL: Well, your dance company for...

CHLOE: (*interrupts*) I don't want...

VAL: (*interrupts*) The house. I'm done with it.

CHLOE: I was going to give up everything to be here. This is crazy.

LISA: Yeah, you can't sell now, mum.

VAL: I think I can decide that.

LISA: Listen, the market, it's rubbish right now. We can't get a buyer for our house and that's Colchester. God knows, what it's going to be like here.

CHLOE: And the house is in a dreadful state!

VAL: Excuse me, love!

CHLOE: The back needs painting, the plumbing...

LISA: You're right.

CHLOE: We can't afford all the repairs now, MV.

LISA: No, we'd end up giving a shocking discount and the sale price won't buy you anywhere else.

VAL: There's no mortgage.

CHLOE: Estate agents fees are crippling.

VAL: I'll get somewhere.

LISA: If we take our time, wait for the market to go up, it's not like we're in the red, we'll get some money in, start on the repairs...

VAL: I don't know.

LISA: Who's it on with?

VAL: Connells.

LISA: We'll give them a call, put it off the market and then we can have a proper chat about it.

CHLOE: I'll get the number.

VAL: I got the number. (*pause*) No, I made my decision.

CHLOE: MV, it's our home.

VAL: Is it about the money?

LISA: No one's thinking about money.

CHLOE: No... when I was little... here... the stories you'd tell me. A family of ten all in one room, Great Nan's fish pie, everyone watches the news in the lounge...

VAL: Are you drunk?

CHLOE: The places we played...

LISA: Hiding behind the dresser in the lounge. The den under the breakfast bar.

CHLOE: How do you...?

LISA: Kids all play the same games. (*beat*) Think about it, mum.

VAL: (*to Lisa*) You wanted to burn this place down, love. Do you remember?

LISA: That's the past.

VAL: Yes.

CHLOE: You're throwing us out.

VAL: What did you say?

CHLOE: Where are we going to go?

VAL: The house won't sell overnight, sweetheart.

CHLOE: Where?

VAL: Like what Lisa said, the sale will take a while. You can stay here as long as what you want while we're waiting.

CHLOE: I've got nowhere to go.

VAL: I could do with your help. Same as with Lisa.

CHLOE: Don't sell!

VAL: Chloe!

CHLOE: Mummy Val... please!

VAL: (*pause*) No.

CHLOE: Please!

VAL: I'm going to bed.

LISA: What about the tree? We was...

VAL: (*interrupts*) I don't care about the tree.

LISA: Don't say that!

VAL: You can burn it down for all I care.

LISA: No!

CHLOE: MV!

(*Val exits*)

LISA: We was getting on. Her and me.

CHLOE: Shit!

LISA: I'm changing things round here, Chloe. The town's still quiet...

CHLOE: Dead!

LISA: But I'd like to try. That's all. (*pause*) I don't know what's got into her.

9 MEMORY: CHLOE GOES TO UNIVERSITY, 2012

Chloe in the car with Val. Lisa in a separate space writing a card for Chloe.

LISA: It's 2012 and I'm 36. I got a job and a husband and a daughter.

CHLOE: It is 2012 and I am going to London to study contemporary dance and we can't get all my stuff in the car and MV's worried about my driving even though it was her idea to hire the car and she's coming with me and I'm a confident driver.

LISA: I got her a card. (*beat*) A good luck card.

CHLOE: And on the journey she's fretting about this and that and what I've forgotten to take and I say, 'they do have shops in London, MV!' and she laughs. And we're both laughing. And then she says that Grandad would be proud and she tells me the story about him dancing in front of the West Cliff and people missing the start of the show because they're watching him. And I've heard this story a 100 times, a 1000 times, a bloody million times but this time... I'm watching the road, not looking at her face... this time it's like I've never heard this story before. (*beat*) And I want to ask her why she tells it so much. (*beat*) She says Grandad would have been proud. She says it's like we've gone full circle. And I don't know what she's on about but it's raining outside and we're warm and excited and she's made fairy cakes and I know I'm going miss her. (*beat*) Her, the house, Clacton, her. (*pause*)

LISA: I write good luck. Then I write I'll miss you. (*beat*) Then I cross it out. Because it ain't true because I see her so little. (*beat*) I miss her every day. I can't miss her anymore. It'll just be missing her in a different place. Where is... It's not the distance, the miles. No, it's... it's not being here. She's not here with me. (*beat*) I'm not going to send it. No. (*beat*) She's been gone a long time. (*beat, loudly*) I'm not going to send it.

10. GUESTHOUSE, quarters, DEC 2017, (early eve)

Continued from 8.

CHLOE: We should call them.

LISA: What?

CHLOE: The Estate Agents. Get them to put if off the market.

LISA: We can't do that.

CHLOE: Why not…?

LISA: Because it's her house. They won't take instructions from us.

CHLOE: If we explain she's unwell. It's all so local here, they'll probably know about her accident. We can say it's temporary until she fully recovers.

LISA: No, no, that's…

CHLOE: We're giving her a chance.

LISA: Yeah. (*beat*) Yeah. Alright. We'll do it. Sometimes… you, yeah. (*beat*) Do you want to give them a call?

CHLOE: Me?

LISA: It's your idea.

CHLOE: It's your idea to put it off the market in the first place.

LISA: Chloe, are you going to make the call?

CHLOE: (*pause*) No. I can't… I

LISA: No.

CHLOE: (*laughing*) It's Christmas Eve! We can't call them now!

LISA: No. (*pause*)

CHLOE: Will she go through with it?

LISA: I don't know. We'll get her to change her mind.

CHLOE: How?

LISA: What she said. We'll stay here, get things in good shape. Then she'll lose interest in selling and...

CHLOE: (*interrupts*) She won't lose interest.

LISA: If we stay in the black, get the numbers up. There's two of us. We can manage the house and...

CHLOE: (*interrupts*) I don't want to manage it.

LISA: But you said...

CHLOE: Yeah I know.

LISA: Chloe, I thought you liked it here.

CHLOE: I don't want to live here forever. Nor do you.

LISA: Yes I do. I don't know about forever, I...

CHLOE: (*interrupts*) You're hiding. Like me.

LISA: Hiding?

CHLOE: And I don't want to run a dance company

LISA: I thought that was your plan.

CHLOE: Her plan.

LISA: But... you always loved to dance, Chloe. That time I saw you in Colchester, the smile on your face...

CHLOE: (*interrupts*) I was a kid performing.

LISA: You was loving it, you was happy.

CHLOE: Yeah I was always happy. (*beat*) I didn't know you were allowed to be anything else. (*beat*) I wanted to please her.

LISA: Yeah. (*beat*) Chloe, I... I didn't want to be invisible.

CHLOE: What?

LISA: All that time. When you was growing up, and you was here with mum, and I was...

CHLOE: I'm not listening to this.

LISA: Chloe, please.

CHLOE: I'm not listening.

LISA: I didn't...

CHLOE: You abandoned me!

LISA: No I never.

CHLOE: Yes you did!

LISA: No, no. Not like that. (*calling after Chloe*) Chloe! Chloe! Don't... (*to self*) I wanted you.

ACT 2.

1. MEMORY: CLACTON REC, 1979

Val is pushing Lisa on a swing.

VAL: It's 1979 and she's beautiful. I'm pushing her on the swings down the rec and She is giggling and screaming, 'Higher, Mummy, higher!' You'd think it was the Stella down the pier. (*as if talking to child*) 'Watch out, sweetie!' 'There you go!' (*pause*) She is a dream, this one, and sometimes when we go for our walk, I feel like I am dreaming. (*beat*) We come here all the time, even when it's raining, it's too nippy down the front this time of year and she loves to swing. We get out every day if we can, after hot lunch and before check in, if he's not on a job, which is most often because the work's not what it was, (*beat*) or if he's not on the drink. (*pause*)

Sometimes I think he's getting worse, and other times I don't know, and sometimes I don't even mind. We're still making money and that's something. I tell him it's his inheritance. (*beat*) But he says he's hemmed in, can't escape. He's been stuck here all his life, he says. A prison sentence. (*beat*) He likes talking to the guests, doing a turn in the lounge, he likes the applause, makes him feel special. (*beat*) He don't like much else. (*to baby*) 'But he loves you! You're his little precious!' (*beat*) I say to him, so where do you want to escape to? He says, I wouldn't understand.

2. GUESTHOUSE, Val's quarters, DEC 2017, (later on Christmas Eve)

Lisa enters, shaking, pacing around, Val enters.

VAL: Lis, what are you doing? (*pause*) Lisa?

LISA: I'm alright.

VAL: Well you don't look it. I heard you girls fighting when I went to bed. What's going on?

LISA: (*with difficulty*) I can't sleep. There.

VAL: I put you in No 4 because I needed the double. What you doing down here?

LISA: No. I… no.

VAL: I don't know what's wrong with No 4. You've got an en suite in there now. They've all got en suites. What people want these days. When we took over, there was one bathroom for the house, then we had one per floor, and now…

LISA: I can't sleep up there.

VAL: And now every room.

LISA: I can't…

VAL: And you get the sun of a morning.

LISA: (*shouting*) No!

VAL: Lis, are you not on your tranqs?

LISA: (*quietly*) No.

VAL: How about another port and lemon? (*Lisa shakes her head*) A little digestif and you'll be…

LISA: Can I sleep here?

VAL: I don't want to be making up the sofa bed now. All my linen's upstairs.

LISA: It's safe here.

VAL: I don't want to be funny, love, but is this some sort of game because you ain't got what you want?

LISA: No.

VAL: Do you think I'm going to change my mind? Because bellyaching about where you're going to sleep is not going to…

LISA: (*interrupts*) Him! (*beat*) I keep thinking about him.

VAL: What, you're missing Markie?

LISA: Dad! (*pause*)

VAL: Before… before I asked you here, I… (*beat*) I wanted to give you a chance, seeing as you'd offered, and you done good, but…

LISA: (*interrupts*) When he died, I was upstairs.

VAL: Yes, your old room.

LISA: And you didn't come. (*beat*) After… when I cried…

VAL: What?

LISA: You don't come.

VAL: Yes I did. You was always having nightmares, I'd be worried you'd wake the guests. I used to throw cold water over you.

LISA: I hate you. Doing that…

VAL: I had to do something to...

LISA: (*speaking over her*) I hate you.

VAL: Lis...

LISA: Get away from me.

VAL: Lis!

LISA: Is he cold?

VAL: What?

LISA: In the water. Is he cold?

VAL: Stop...

LISA: (*speaking over her*) You can jump the waves.

VAL: Stop it!

LISA: And sing. He likes to sing. (*sings*)

VAL: Stop that now!

LISA: Don't stop singing, Dad.

VAL: Stop! Stop! Stop!

LISA: Get out of the water! Quick! Quick!

VAL: Calm down!

LISA: You got to be quick! Dad! Dad! Dad!

VAL: Lisa!!! (*shakes Lisa,*) Calm down! (*pause, Lisa calms down*)

LISA: Why did you...?

VAL: I had to get you out of it.

LISA: (*pause*) I would have stopped him.

VAL: It's over, Lisa. (*hugs her as if hugging a child*)

LISA: Mum.

VAL: It's over. (*pause*)

LISA: I shouldn't have come back here. When you invited me... I was... I was over the moon. But... this place. I wanted to help. Things change and I... I thought I... maybe you're right. I should go. I'll go now. (*pause, Lisa seems about to leave*)

VAL: Lis!

LISA: No point hanging about.

VAL: Don't be silly, love. It's Christmas Day. Where you going to go?

LISA: I still got the house.

VAL: You want to spend Christmas Day on your own?

LISA: No.

VAL: Well then.

LISA: I just... I... I... Dad. (*pause*)

VAL: Sometimes you screamed and I come running up. 'Don't wake the guests!' The noise! Other times... that's why I put you up there. (*beat*) I didn't want to hear your cries. If I didn't hear them, I could pretend... that he was still alive.

LISA: He was dead.

VAL: (*beat*) Yes.

LISA: And you wouldn't talk to me

VAL: I had to get on - the guests, the business, everyone else going under, end of Butlins, debts, fear of repossession – you wouldn't have known what that meant. I protected you. Yes, I did. After your Dad... I had to be practical. (*beat*) We survived, didn't we?

LISA: You was ashamed.

VAL: No.

LISA: You was ashamed of him, and later you was ashamed of me.

VAL: I kept you alive.

LISA: No you never.

VAL: Without me...

LISA: (*interrupts*) Dad kept me alive. And you still pretend. (*pause*) I'll get off.

VAL: It's the middle of the night.

LISA: I like driving in the dark.

VAL: I don't want you to go.

LISA: I'm going.

VAL: Lisa, please, Lisa. Don't...

LISA: (*interrupts*) I got to go.

VAL: (*shouting after her*) It's not your fault.

LISA: (*trying not to listen*) No.

VAL: Listen to me, love. Listen to me. Listen. It is not your fault. And it never was.

LISA: I was...

VAL: His special girl.

LISA: I wasn't enough.

VAL: It's not your fault. (*beat*) I had to keep going, sweetheart.

LISA: Yeah, you said...

VAL: (*interrupts*) I never wanted to. No. But you got to keep moving. Time don't stop, only in your head. But the clock's always ticking, racing ahead. You cover up the cracks and you move on.

LISA: You said nothing.

VAL: You were growing up, you needed stuff. School shoes, ballet lessons.

LISA: A mum.

VAL: Stuff. (*beat*) Every other guesthouse was crumbling to dust, I stood up tall. I kept on going. For you. I had to be clever, dream up ideas, going upmarket, diversifying, we never took no mentals like everywhere else. (*beat*) I kept you alive. (*pause*) Shall I get you a blanket?

LISA: (*hesitates*) Yeah. I'll...

VAL: Go make yourself something hot, I got ovaltine, cocoa.

LISA: Yeah. (*exits*)

3. MEMORY: GUESTHOUSE, Val's quarters, MARCH 1996

Val is waiting anxiously.

VAL: It is 2017.

(*Lisa enters with suitcases/bags*)

LISA: It is 1996.

(*pause*)

VAL: Goodness me, love, looks like you've bought the university library with you? Couldn't you have left some of this with your pals. Put it in storage? A locker? Don't they give you a locker?

LISA: No.

VAL: Seems silly to me. You'll have to cart all this back with you after the...

LISA: (*interrupts*) Back...?

VAL: When you go back, love. But don't think about that now. You got six weeks off. You're home now, that's the thing.

LISA: Home!

VAL: Yes, and the weather's lovely. The daffs are getting quite excited outside. We'll go for a stroll later. (*beat*) You won't believe this but some of the guests have been in the sea already.

LISA: No.

VAL: I know. Scandinavian types I think. Definitely foreign.

LISA: I don't like the sea.

VAL: I'm not asking you to get your cossie out.

LISA: The waves.

VAL: You need a nice rest, love, and then once you get sorted…

LISA: (*interrupts*) No.

VAL: What do you mean no?

LISA: I don't know.

VAL: You'll be right as rain in six weeks. You'll see. Give it a few days and you'll be getting itchy feet, desperate to see your pals again.

LISA: No.

VAL: So what else do you think you're going to do here? Serve up full English with a smile on your face? Get your hands dirty, getting stuck into room service?

LISA: Chloe…?

VAL: She's fine.

LISA: Is she…?

VAL: Yes, she's used to you being away now.

LISA: Is she…?

VAL: She's asleep. It's eight o'clock. Out like a light, bless her!

LISA: Can I…?

VAL: I said she's asleep. (*beat*) You'll see her in the morning. She's up before me. Helps me out with breakfast. A treasure she is. Now do you want a cuppa? (*beat*) I were guessing you'd have got yourself a sandwich on the train, but I made us a spot of cake, if you fancy it, be out in a minute …

LISA: Mum….

VAL: Victoria sandwich. You can have a nice big piece. We need to get your strength up.

LISA: Chloe…?

VAL: We don't want you wasting away. You're looking skinny enough…

LISA: I need to see her.

VAL: Yes love, we discussed that, didn't we? In the morning…

LISA: Now.

VAL: Shhh! Lisa!

LISA: Please!

VAL: Don't you think you've caused enough trouble? You was alright at Christmas. A good first term you had, passed all your whatsits.

LISA: Modular tests.

VAL: Yes, that's what the professor said. He called me personally. He thinks you'd benefit from a medical assessment. 'A psychiatrist,' he said. I went all quiet on the phone. 'A doctor who will diagnose mental disorder', he goes. I said, 'I am familiar with the term. Have you been to Clacton, love?' I said, 'We're full of nutters here, it's where they dump 'em.' (*beat*) He went all quiet then. (*beat*) Thinks I'm some mean hearted cow.

LISA: You wanted me to go.

VAL: Go where?

LISA: There.

VAL: What, to university? Course I did. (*beat*) Do you think it's easy for me? Do you? Running this place with next to no staff and running round after Chloe? She's easy as they go but they're all handfuls, terrible twos, you was...

LISA: I want to see her.

VAL: Will you keep your voice down!

LISA: PLEASE!

VAL: Lisa!

LISA: I'm her mum.

VAL: Course you are. I'm Mummy Val.

LISA: What?

VAL: Just what she calls me. Mum, mum, mum she goes, like they do. I'm Mummy Val, I say. (*beat*) I don't want her getting confused.

LISA: About what?

VAL: Well... just confused. (*pause*) What do you expect love?

LISA: I'm not going back.

VAL: Yes you are, you...

LISA: No. (*beat*) I want Dad.

VAL: (*beat*) He's not here.

LISA: No. (*beat*) I'm going to Chloe.

VAL: Don't you dare… Lisa!

LISA: (*exits, shouting*) Chloe!

4. GUESTHOUSE, DEC 2017, (following morning)

Val is anxious, Lisa enters.

VAL: Morning, love.

LISA: Morning.

VAL: Happy Christmas! (*tries to hug Lisa*)

LISA: (*pushing Val away*) I got a stiff neck.

VAL: Sorry, I...

LISA: It's alright.

VAL: I told you that sofa's a killer.

LISA: Yeah.

VAL: I'm glad you're here.

LISA: Yeah.

VAL: Meanwhile she's still sulking.

LISA: What?

VAL: Chloe. (*pause*) She's sulking and you're getting your hands dirty. (*beat*) I heard you up nice and early even though you had a bad night. Getting the rooms done before breakfast, was you?

LISA: Yeah, and wrapping presents.

VAL: We'll do them after lunch. (*pause*) I can't believe we still got guests. Christmas Day! Last year it was just me and Chloe and the ghosts.

LISA: I would have come.

VAL: Well, you come on Boxing Day, like you do. (*beat*) What is it, love? Do you want a cup of tea?

LISA: I want her back.

VAL: Yes, I never seen her sulking before. (*beat*) She was never one for tantrums. (*beat*) I never said no to her. I spoilt her. That's the thing. That's what you do when you're a Nan, you spoil 'em.

LISA: She's gone.

VAL: What are you on about…?

LISA: She's gone.

VAL: Love, she's upstairs in bed, sleeping like a baby last time I had a…

LISA: (*interrupts*) A baby.

VAL: Lisa…

LISA: There's nothing. Nothing for me.

VAL: Have you been mixing alcohol with your meds?

LISA: Chloe!

VAL: Is this about the house again? You don't want me selling it? (*pause*) I know you're set on it but I got your interests at heart. The both of you. (*pause*) I don't want you getting old here, wasting your life away, trying to sell holidays in a town that's past its sell by date. (*beat*) I want you to live your life.

LISA: It's too late.

VAL: Too late! You're what? Forty two! Too late! What are you about? You'll be alright. Yes, you will. I've seen what you're made of now. You got more of my genes than your Dad's after all.

LISA: I got fifty fifty.

VAL: Oh it's more complex than that, love. Genetic inheritance. I saw a programme on Sky. (*beat*) Now, do you want to check she's alright?

LISA: She don't love me.

VAL: Save my legs. (*pause*) Righto, I'll give her a shout. (*moves to one side*) Chloe!

LISA: She don't love me.

VAL: Well... in her own way. Course she does. You're her mum.

LISA: You brought her up.

VAL: Oh and did I have a choice?

LISA: You stopped her loving me.

VAL: Now stop that, you can stop right there, madam. What a thing to... how dare you?

LISA: It's true.

VAL: I'm tired, Lisa.

LISA: You sent me away.

VAL: To study, to make a life for yourself, so you could support her.

LISA: (*speaking over her*) After. To that place.

VAL: You was ill. I was protecting you, and Chloe. I was protecting her from you.

LISA: No.

VAL: If you want the truth.

LISA: Will you tell her about Dad?

VAL: What?

LISA: The truth?

VAL: About him shouting all the time? Shouting the house down, smashing bottles, waking up the guests...

LISA: (*interrupts*) He didn't shout at me.

VAL: What so you didn't hear him?

LISA: I didn't like him doing it.

VAL: (*pause*) No.

LISA: Will you tell her?

(*Chloe enters*)

VAL: Chloe!

CHLOE: Merry Christmas, MV!

VAL: And the same to you, sweetheart.

LISA: Merry Christmas, Chloe.

VAL: Now what time do you call this?

CHLOE: I don't know. Morning.

VAL: 11.30?

CHLOE: Yeah that is morning.

VAL: Not in my book. Good job, you're not on roasts today.

CHLOE: When...

VAL: It's alright. Lisa's on it.

LISA: Should be out for 1.

VAL: (*to Chloe*) You look terrible!

CHLOE: There's a man in my head with a hammer.

VAL: Oh, get her some paracetamol, Lisa, and a fizzy water.

CHLOE: I just want a coffee.

VAL: Lisa?

LISA: (*staring at Chloe, not listening to Val*) Yeah.

VAL: (*to Chloe*) Well, I'll do it then. I know how you like it. (*exits*)

LISA: How you...?

CHLOE: Awful!

LISA: Yeah.

CHLOE: Yesterday, look, I was drunk and..

LISA: I don't want to live here forever. You're right. (*beat*) But I aint scared.

CHLOE: Scared?

LISA: To be here.

CHLOE: Tom used to get scared when I came down.

LISA: What?

CHLOE: All those documentaries. He worried about me getting stabbed.

LISA: But you live in London...?

CHLOE: Yeah! (*they laugh*)(*pause*)

LISA: Are you... with him...?

CHLOE: I'm good. (*beat*) It's not like he's my first boyfriend.

LISA: First bloke you lived with.

CHLOE: That wasn't living. (*beat*) I don't know how to live.

LISA: What...?

CHLOE: Sometimes it feels hard. That's all. (*beat*) Yesterday... I was drunk and... I didn't want to upset you. When you're drunk, you say stuff and... and you can't even remember what you said.

LISA: But you remember what I said? (*beat*) Don't you? (*beat*) I wanted you, Chloe. (*beat*) I wanted you... I did, but I couldn't... I was... It was like I weren't in the world no more. How could I have looked after you? I couldn't look after myself.

CHLOE: But you got better.

LISA: And then I wanted you back.

CHLOE: Yeah.

LISA: (*loudly*) I wanted you back. (*pause*) We got you a swing in the garden me and Mark. And a My Little Pony duvet set. We was going to take it slowly – start with you coming to play, then staying over at a weekend. (*beat*) You'd seen so much, we didn't want to rush you.

CHLOE: You're lying.

LISA: You liked coming at first. Mark pushed you high on the swing.

CHLOE: I can't remember.

LISA: One day you wouldn't get in the car. (*beat*) You wouldn't come.

CHLOE: And you gave up on me!

LISA: You was so upset. Screaming and kicking like a toddler. (*beat*) We stopped the visits. (*beat*) She thought it was for the best.

CHLOE: Don't blame MV!

LISA: She made the decision. She thought you'd be better off with her.

CHLOE: And what did you think?

LISA: I thought she was right. (*beat*) No, no I was scared.

CHLOE: Of MV?

LISA: Of you. Of messing it up with you. (*pause*) I'm sorry.

CHLOE: Sorry!

LISA: Yes!

CHLOE: All my life and you're not there. And now you're sorry. You know, I never minded not having a Dad because no one had a Dad round here or if they had he was most likely some lazy bastard who couldn't get a job. (*beat*) I minded about you.

LISA: Sorry, I... I don't... what else...? I don't know what else to say.

CHLOE: (*interrupts*) I don't want you to say anything.

(*Val enters*)

VAL: (*to Chloe*) So I got your coffee, sweetheart.

LISA: (*to Val*) Will you tell her mum, now, please.

CHLOE: (*to Lisa*) Tell me what?

LISA: (*to Val*) All of it.

VAL: (*ignoring Lisa, to Chloe*) Will you get that down you?

LISA: I'll tell her.

VAL: No.

CHLOE: Tell me what?

LISA: Yeah, I will.

CHLOE: MV?

VAL: No.

CHLOE: Do you think her sugar...?

LISA: (*interrupts*) No.

VAL: (*to Lisa*) We always said the past was over.

LISA: But it ain't. (*pause*)

VAL: I went down the pier when he ended it.

CHLOE: What?

VAL: Yes I did. As soon as they told me. (*to Lisa*) You was asleep, bless you. (*beat*) I wanted to see the spot where he... where... (*pause*) It was dark when I got there. And I was thinking, was it dark when he jumped? I didn't like that, you see. Well, I've never liked the pier in the dark, no. I wanted it to be light. (*pause*) I kept the note. Yes I did. For weeks after. It had roses on it. Oh he hadn't drawn them, it was the design. From this floral notebook I kept on the sideboard.

CHLOE: What's she...?

VAL: (*talking over Chloe*) But he could have written it on the back of an envelope and he didn't and I liked that. I liked to think he was being thoughtful. We had roses at our wedding, see.

CHLOE: Grandad...?

VAL: Oh I knew it couldn't bring him back, the note, but when he wrote it... he was alive. Or was he already dead? I mean dead on the inside. You can breathe and you can smile, you can run a guesthouse shipshape, but you can still be dead on the inside.

CHLOE: No, this is...

LISA: It's alright, Chloe.

CHLOE: No it's not.

LISA: Well, no...

CHLOE: It is not alright.

VAL: (*to Chloe*) I'm sorry, sweetheart.

CHLOE: (*to Val*) You told me... you...

VAL: I said it was his heart. That were a lie.

CHLOE: Why..?

VAL: Only in some ways it weren't. Because if you could feel your heart, you wouldn't do it, would you? When someone does something like that it's like a sickness of the heart and...

CHLOE: (*interrupts*) Why didn't you tell me?

LISA: She's told you now.

CHLOE: Before. MV, why... why...?

VAL: Before you was born.

CHLOE: So.

VAL: So you didn't need to know. That's what I thought. I thought you don't need to know.

CHLOE: No, that's... I should have... you should have...

VAL: (*interrupts*) And to protect you. We wanted to protect you.

LISA: I didn't want to...

CHLOE: (*interrupts, to Val*) From what?

VAL: The world.

LISA: Chloe...

CHLOE: Leave me alone! (*pause*)

LISA: I wanted Mum to tell you, Chloe. (*pause*) Chloe, will you look at me?

CHLOE: I can't...

LISA: I wanted you to know. Maybe I was wrong. I get everything wrong, don't I? But I thought, if you knew... if you knew...

CHLOE: What do you expect?

LISA: ...We could talk about it. (*pause*)

VAL: I were angry too.

CHLOE: I'm not angry.

LISA: We got to talk about it.

VAL: With Bri. I used to speak to him in my head like I do. 'How could you, Bri?' 'How could you do it?' (*quietly*)

Why wasn't we good enough? (*pause*) Oh I don't know if he loved me, not by then, (*to Lisa*) but he loved you. His little precious. You was his world, what he used to say.

LISA: I know.

VAL: And maybe I was once. Or maybe I was dreaming. (*pause*) I wouldn't talk to you after... I was deluding myself, you see. I had to, to keep afloat... I couldn't look you in the eye, could I?

LISA: No.

VAL: You was a kid and suddenly you can't sit on his knee or hear him singing in the bath. (*pause*) And there was this silence between me and you. You needed answers.

LISA: It's alright, mum.

VAL: (*pause*) At night I pretended I didn't hear you crying. 'Everyone has nightmares,' I'd say. (*pause*) When you had the breakdown, it was too late.

(*pause. Lisa looks at Chloe.*)

CHLOE: (*to Lisa*) The visits. To your place.

LISA: Chloe!

CHLOE: (*pause*) I never wanted them to stop. (*pause*) I don't know why I screamed. I never wanted them to stop.

5. MEMORY: CHLOE VISITS LISA, 1999

Chloe and Lisa are in separate spaces. Chloe is on the train to Lisa's house. Lisa is in her kitchen, waiting for Chloe and Val.

LISA: It's 1999 and they're coming here.

CHLOE: It's 1999 and I'm six and we're on the train to Lisa's.

VAL: It's 1999 and I keep her close.

LISA: Both of them.

VAL: You've got to on the train, these days. Yes you have.

CHLOE: And I been to Colchester before, but not her house because she comes to us because we're too busy, but we done the shops. Yeah, they got better ones than us but we got Marks too and MV loves Marks but I don't, but sometimes I get sweets or a comic.

VAL: I get her a comic to read on the train but she aint reading it.

LISA: When I told mum, it's like she thinks I'm grown up now or something.

CHLOE: I like looking out of the window. We're at Thorpe now. It's where you live if you're posh but not as posh as Frinton.

LISA: And she's all, 'have you got a list, love?' Same as what the staff keep asking in the staff room. 'What do you want?' 'What can we get you?'

VAL: I keep looking at her.

CHLOE: MV keeps looking at me, 'MV, what is it?'

LISA: But I don't want nothing. I want her to come. With Chloe. And that's it.

VAL: And then I tell her.

CHLOE: (*whispers*) and then she tells me a secret. (*loudly*) Lisa is getting married to Mark.

LISA: I tell her I don't need a list, 'Mark's got everything, mum, ain't he?' Then she goes, 'has he got a gravy boat?' and I'm like, 'yeah we don't do gravy.' And she says, 'well, how about the roast?' And I say we don't do a roast usually on a Sunday. (*beat*) She goes quiet like she does and I explain that Mark does rugby Sundays and I've always got stuff for school… (*beat*) Then she says Chloe likes a roast and I'm saying, well, yeah if Chloe was here, if we was a family…

VAL: I told Lisa I wouldn't say anything but I don't want Chloe getting all upset.

CHLOE: (*quieter*) Yeah, it's true, and I'm surprised because he's her friend and you don't marry your friends, that's against the law, but it turns out he's also her boyfriend at the same time and you can marry your boyfriend. It's allowed.

LISA: They're coming, there's the thing. They're coming and she's pleased and…

VAL: It's best coming from me.

CHLOE: A wedding! (*beat*) 'MV, can I be a bridesmaid?'

LISA: I want her to be a bridesmaid.

VAL: She wants to be a bridesmaid.

CHLOE: MV says it's not that sort of a wedding. But I never heard of a wedding with no bridesmaids so I want to know what sort of a wedding it is.

LISA: My wedding!

VAL: I don't want to talk about the wedding.

CHLOE: She won't say no more so I say I'm going to ask Lisa.

VAL: I look at her.

CHLOE: MV looks at me.

LISA: I keep looking at the clock. Have I got everything ready? I got some orange fizz for Chloe, Mr Kipling cakes for mum, beer for Mark, it'll be a bit of a do, a celebration.

VAL: We find the house alright. Number 8 bus from North station. Her bloke, fiancé – would you believe – he offered a lift but I said no. Well I've never met him and although he sounds decent, with Lisa's track record…

LISA: I see them coming from inside.

CHLOE: Outside the house, MV stops, and I'm impatient.

VAL: Outside the house, I stop. Not to look at it. No. They're all the same these new builds, no character, but… I'm shaking.

CHLOE: MV looks weird. 'Come on, MV!'

VAL: My legs go all jelly and I'm gripping Chloe's hand.

CHLOE: She's squeezing my hand and it's hurting and I don't know why.

VAL: And I don't even know why.

CHLOE: 'Let go, MV.'

VAL: Why I'm stopping and shaking… why I can't let go.

(*pause*)

CHLOE: We're in the garden and I like it here.

LISA: I watch them in the garden.

VAL: I watch them in the garden.

CHLOE: Mark says he'll build me a swing one day and I say, 'Can we do it now?' And he says next time and I say, 'When?' and he says whenever I like, and I want to do it tomorrow. And now he's smiling at me.

LISA: And I think I made a good choice.

VAL: And I think, well he's quite good with her.

CHLOE: I ain't got a garden at home because we got the beach and that's better. But I like it here, this garden, there's roses and you don't get those down the beach. (*beat*) I smile back at Mark and he's still smiling and I know why.

LISA: And she's smiling.

VAL: He's a teacher of course. It's what you'd expect.

CHLOE: Because I know his secret.

LISA: But I got to tell her.

CHLOE: When Lisa tells me, she don't look at me.

LISA: I don't know why I feel so nervous.

CHLOE: She like looks through me like I'm invisible because she never looks at me.

LISA: When I tell her, she's not that excited. She don't look excited. She might… It'll be a shock to her. Like what Mum said. She don't say much.

CHLOE: I got so many questions.

LISA: She don't ask nothing. No questions. I don't know – the cake, bridesmaids, honeymoon, none of that.

CHLOE: But MV says I got to be polite.

VAL: I tell her to be polite.

LISA: She'll get used to it. And Mum's pleased and that's... that's something.

VAL: He seems nice enough and the house is ship shape. I start to think I've taught her something after all. And she's done a lovely spread. All shop bought from the Tescos Superstore round the corner but I do like a Mr Kipling and she was never that light with her sponge.

CHLOE: 'That's lovely,' I say.

LISA: And it's not like she got upset about it or nothing.

VAL: Nothing needs to change. Lisa'll be married and that's a good thing.

CHLOE: And then I say, 'Can I be a bridesmaid?' I do. I actually say it. (*pause*)

LISA: Before Mark proposed, I never wanted to get married.

VAL: And I don't want it to. I don't want it to change.

CHLOE: I say it in my head.

VAL: But seeing her in the garden with Markie, I'm thinking yes he's very good with her really. (*beat*) Like Bri was with Lisa. Before... Like a Dad. Like a proper Dad. (*beat*) I don't want things to change but... she needs... maybe... (*beat*) They got a house and a car and jobs and maybe... she needs... but I want... maybe one day... all of us... one day.

CHLOE: I say it to Grandad.

VAL: I tell her to get her coat and shoes.

CHLOE: I get my coat and shoes.

LISA: I wave them goodbye.

All: And I think about next time.

LISA: One day.

CHLOE: All of us.

VAL: Maybe.

END